AR pts
0.5

Kyle Massey

cing
he stars

ABDO
Publishing Company

Big
Buddy BOOKS
Buddy Bios

by Sarah Tieck

Published by ABDO Publishing Company, 8000 West 78th Street, Edina, Minnesota 55439.

Printed in the United States of America, North Mankato, Minnesota.
062011
092011
 PRINTED ON RECYCLED PAPER

Coordinating Series Editor: Rochelle Baltzer
Contributing Editors: Megan M. Gunderson, BreAnn Rumsch, Marcia Zappa
Graphic Design: Maria Hosley
Cover Photograph: *AP Photo*: Chris Pizzello.
Interior Photographs/Illustrations: *AP Photo*: Michal Czerwonka/PictureGroup via AP IMAGES (p. 17), Phelan M. Ebenhack (p. 15), Jennifer Graylock (pp. 10, 15), Charles Sykes (pp. 4, 23); *Getty Images*: Jean-Paul Aussenard/ WireImage (p. 9), Disney Channel/Disney Channel via Getty Images (p. 22), Jesse Grant (p. 12), Frazer Harrison (p. 17), Iris/WireImage (p. 7), Adam Larkey/ABC via Getty Images (p. 21), Matthew Peyton (p. 11), Tiffany Rose/WireImage (p. 29), Stephen Shugerman (p. 27), Paul Warner/WireImage for Future US (pp. 19, 25).

Library of Congress Cataloging-in-Publication Data

Tieck, Sarah, 1976-
  Kyle Massey : talented entertainer / Sarah Tieck.
    p. cm. -- (Big buddy biographies) (Rising star -- Family ties -- A young actor -- Big break -- New opportunities -- Music man -- Lights! camera! action! -- Dancing star -- An actor's life -- Off the screen -- Buzz.)
  ISBN 978-1-61783-019-8
  1. Massey, Kyle, 1991---Juvenile literature. 2. Actors--United States--Biography--Juvenile literature. 3. Singers-- United States--Biography--Juvenile literature. I. Title.
  PN2287.M5427T54 2011
  791.4302'8092--dc23
  [B]
                                    2011018231

Kyle Massey

Contents

Rising Star

Kyle Massey is an actor and a **rapper**. He is known for starring in the television shows *That's So Raven* and *Cory in the House*. And, he has **released** popular rap music.

Tennessee

North Carolina

Atlanta ☆

South Carolina

Alabama   Georgia

Florida

ATLANTIC OCEAN

GULF OF MEXICO

N
W   E
S

Family Ties

Kyle Orlando Massey was born in Atlanta, Georgia, on August 28, 1991. Kyle's parents are Angel and Michael Massey. His older brother is named Christopher.

GET READY FOR MUSH HOUR!

GET READY

As kids, Kyle (*left*) and his brother had fun attending events together.

7

A Young Actor

Kyle grew up in Atlanta. People first noticed Kyle's talent when he was young. He was discovered while waiting for his brother to audition for a role! Soon after, Kyle appeared in a play of *The Wizard of Oz.*

Kyle enjoyed acting. Soon, he began working as a professional actor. He earned small parts on television shows and in commercials.

Kyle and Christopher were both working actors at a young age.

9

Big Break

Around 2002, Kyle **auditioned** for a Disney Channel show called *That's So Raven*. He got a big **role**!

The show is about Raven Baxter, a teenager who can see the **future**. Her special skill leads to lots of fun adventures! On the show, Kyle played Raven's little brother, Cory Baxter.

Raven-Symoné played the main character on *That's So Raven*.

On *That's So Raven*, Kyle (*right*) worked with Anneliese van der Pol (*left*) and Orlando Brown (*center*). They played Raven's friends.

In 2008, *That's So Raven* won an NAACP Image Award. These honor excellence in film, television, and music by people of color.

That's So Raven was very popular! It ran from 2003 to 2007. During that time, the show was **nominated** for two Emmy Awards. This was a big honor.

Kyle proved to be a successful actor, too. He won a Young Artist Award for his acting skills in 2007.

New Opportunities

In 2005, Kyle starred in a Disney Channel movie called *Life Is Ruff*. It is about a boy and his dog. Kyle used his musical skills in *Life Is Ruff*. He **rapped** a song called "It's a Dog."

In *Life Is Ruff*, Kyle (*right*) played Calvin Wheeler. Calvin is a popular boy who adopts a dog to win a prize. Actor Mitchel Musso (*left*) played his best friend, Raymond Figg.

Music Man

Aside from acting, Kyle has made his mark in music. He is a talented **rapper** who has **released** several songs.

Kyle's "Underdog Raps" was used in the 2007 movie *Underdog*. And, he rapped the opening song for Disney's *Yin! Yang! Yo!* This short television show ran from 2006 to 2008.

Sometimes Kyle (*left*) raps with his brother (*right*). They formed a music group called the Massey Boyz. They have released songs on the Internet for fans.

Kyle enjoys rapping live.

Lights! Camera! Action!

In 2008, a *Cory in the House* video game came out for Nintendo DS.

In 2007, Kyle began starring in *Cory in the House*. Kyle was excited to get his very own television show!

Kyle played the same character as on *That's So Raven*. But on *Cory in the House*, Cory Baxter moves to the White House. His dad gets a job cooking meals for the US president. Kyle played Cory until the show ended in 2008.

Did you know...

Kyle rapped the opening song for *Cory in the House*.

19

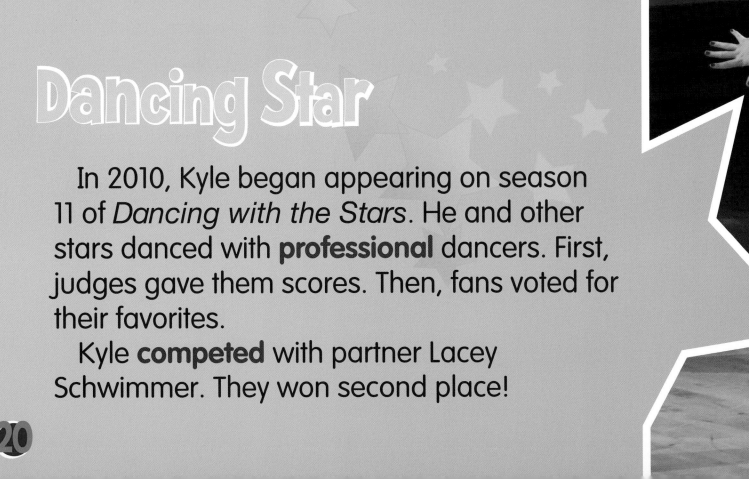

Dancing Star

In 2010, Kyle began appearing on season 11 of *Dancing with the Stars*. He and other stars danced with **professional** dancers. First, judges gave them scores. Then, fans voted for their favorites.

Kyle **competed** with partner Lacey Schwimmer. They won second place!

Dancing is good exercise. Kyle lost nearly 20 pounds (9 kg) while working on *Dancing with the Stars*!

An Actor's Life

Kyle is very busy. In 2010, he began doing cartoon voice work on Disney's *Fish Hooks* television show. He plays the voice of the main character, Milo. And, he has smaller parts on other television shows and in movies.

Did you know...

It is hard for working actors to attend regular school. So, Kyle took online classes with the University of Missouri High School. He completed high school in December 2010.

In *Fish Hooks*, Kyle's character Milo is a teenage fish.

23

Kyle likes to help others. He works with the Starlight Children's Foundation. This group helps sick children and their families.

As an actor, Kyle spends time practicing lines. He also learns songs. He may work on a set for several hours each day.

Sometimes, Kyle travels to attend events and meet fans. His fans are excited to see him!

Off the Screen

When Kyle is not acting, he spends time with friends and family. He enjoys playing sports such as golf and baseball. And, he likes to make music with his brother.

Kyle likes to play games and have fun at events.

Kyle supports groups that help others.

Buzz

In 2011, Kyle began working on a new reality show with his brother. On the show, they live with Bristol Palin in Los Angeles, California. Bristol worked with Kyle on *Dancing with the Stars*.

Kyle's fame continues to grow. People are excited to see what's next for Kyle Massey. Many believe he has a bright **future**!

Snapshot

★**Name**: Kyle Orlando Massey

★**Birthday**: August 28, 1991

★**Birthplace**: Atlanta, Georgia

★**Appearances**: *That's So Raven, Life Is Ruff, Cory in the House, Dancing with the Stars, Fish Hooks*

Important Words

audition (aw-DIH-shuhn) To give a trial performance showcasing personal talent as a musician, a singer, a dancer, or an actor.

commercial (kuh-MUHR-shuhl) a short message on television or radio that helps sell a product.

compete to take part in a contest between two or more persons or groups.

future (FYOO-chuhr) a time that has not yet occurred.

nominate to name as a possible winner.

professional (pruh-FEHSH-nuhl) working for money rather than for pleasure.

rap to speak the words of a song to a beat. A rapper is someone who raps.

release to make available to the public.

role a part an actor plays.

set the place where a movie or a television show is recorded.

Web Sites

To learn more about Kyle Massey, visit ABDO Publishing Company online. Web sites about Kyle Massey are featured on our Book Links page. These links are routinely monitored and updated to provide the most current information available.

www.abdopublishing.com

31

Index